Just Write!

TEN PRACTICAL WORKSHOPS FOR
SUCCESSFUL STUDENT WRITING

Sylvia Gunnery

Pembroke Publishers Limited

For Mom, who praised
my childhood writings,
making the rest possible

©1998 Pembroke Publishers Limited
538 Hood Road
Markham, Ontario L3R 3K9 Canada
1-800-997-9807

Distributed in the U.S. by Stenhouse Publishers
431 York Street,
York, Maine 03909
1-800-988-9812

Canadian Cataloguing in Publication Data

Gunnery, Syliva
   Just write! Ten practical workshops for successful student writing

Includes bibliographical references and index.
ISBN 1-55138-103-6

1. English language — Composition and exercises — Study and teaching (Secondary). I. Title.

LB1631.G86 1998   808'.042'0712   C98-931630-0

Pembroke gratefully acknowledges the support of the Department of Canadian Heritage.

Editor: David Kilgour
Cover Design: John Zehethofer
Cover Photography: Ajay Photographics
Typesetting: Jay Tee Graphics Ltd.

Printed and Bound in Canada
9 8 7 6 5 4 3 2 1

Contents

Introduction

As I've matured, my writing has too. It has grown with me. My stories are a lot longer and more realistic, and my poems have more serious content inside, beneath the ink on the paper.

JULIE (GRADE 9)

It's the beginning of the first term. You and your writing students have months ahead of you to fill . . . with what? The blackboard's clean, notebooks are fresh and empty, pens are ready. There are so many directions to choose from when writers work toward finding meaning, as Julie says, "beneath the ink on the paper."

This book is a collection of ten of those directions you may take in shaping your writing curriculum. I've used them successfully many times in junior and senior high classes. I hope you will find that they work well for you and your students too.

Sylvia Gunnery
Crescent Beach, Nova Scotia
August 1998

CHAPTER 1

Teaching in a writing workshop

The dictionary on my desk needs to be updated because "teach" is defined with these words: instruct; train; impart (give) knowledge. The partnership of teacher and student seems to be diminished by these narrow definitions, especially in the context of a writing workshop. We've evolved from Dickens' image of the Gradgrind teacher brimming with knowledge and pouring it into the empty vessels sitting in row upon row of desks in classrooms.

The writing teacher as a guide

I like to think of all of us in motion. We're exploring, and the teacher is a guide who watches, listens, learns, and advises.

> I'm not an explainer. I am very much an explorer. I don't make the map before I go. I have to trust what I'm hearing or seeing, or what is there, and believe that in putting it down it is going to take the book further into the jungle. Or out the other side. Or however you want to express exploring. Sometimes I find I'm writing scenes and I have no idea where they're going. Absolutely no idea.
>
> TIMOTHY FINDLEY

Each writer chooses a place to go. They want a guide who recognizes the value of their explorations and who will come along on the trip, offering help when needed.

Writers don't want a map to follow, a retracing of the footsteps someone else has made. Was your first trip through the Rockies the same as mine? I was on a midnight train, sitting in the observation car trying to see where the shapes of mountains blocked out the stars. It was exciting for me — like looking for dark and magnificent ghosts. But my "map" through the Rockies wouldn't be one that many would choose to follow.

The writing workshop

I use the term "workshop" loosely — at times I mean an entire class period, but then there are times when only part of a period is enough to keep the momentum going.

In my classroom, students are seated in groups, generally. There are desks and tables which, at times, seem to float, to have an amoeba-like flexibility of shape, as students rearrange the furniture to suit their needs for the day. Maybe there's a larger group discussion, or brief conference with a partner. In a writing workshop, students need time to face each other and talk as well as opportunities for pensive, solitary writing.

There is more to balance as well. Our public school program offers writing — and much more. I try to blend these writing workshops into other aspects of the curriculum: reading, group discussion, drama, research, etc.

The guide as advisor

We want our students to know a lot of things: how to write a full sentence; when a fragment is useful; the correct spelling of thousands of words; the punctuation that best clarifies meaning; when too much is said, or too little; and on and on. In a writing workshop, there are opportunities for all of this to happen.

A mini-lesson, for example, can clarify a particular concept with the whole class. In a fiction workshop where students are experimenting with dialogue, a quick review of the punctuation rules saves the teacher a lot of repeating and correcting. An overhead of an excerpt from a published play can serve as a model when students are beginning to shape their own scripts.

One of the most helpful instruction opportunities comes in a one-on-one exchange between teacher and student. This talk can happen during class time, but, with large class sizes, I have found it easier to turn this exchange into another writing opportunity which I call *I'm wondering...*

When students want my reaction to something they have written or when I want to familiarize myself with what students are doing, I ask that they attach questions to their writing. This is a great time saver and a way of focusing on what is relevant to the writer. No sense talking about plot development yet if the student is still working on the sound of a character's voice.

Nicky is trying her hand at mystery writing and she asks on her *I'm wondering* page: "Are there enough clues to fool you?" and "Underline the first place where you knew how my story would end." Karl is writing about a disappointing father-son relationship and he asks: "In the playground scene, can you tell how much the boy loves his father?"

Every comment I give to writers is careful, whether in a brief note or in conversation. Honesty is crucial. Yet, students are, well... learning. So the criticisms are given for developmental purposes.

A poet, for example, may be passionate about a lost love, yet the emotion smothers the poetry. Here's a note I wrote last week to Carla: "Why is it that we must sometimes feel so much hurt in love? Yet without love, where would joy be? Your poem is one that sets all your true feelings clearly on the page. Good for you. Yet poetry, to be successful, needs to be more distant from the events, perhaps, in order to be more than a straightforward emotional release. There will be a time when you can step back and shape your poem and distill your ideas. Is it too soon to begin? Please let me know if I can help you with your poem."

Comments begin with a reaction to the content and then move towards style and correctness. This makes sense: writers write to say something, not to be corrected by a reader's first reaction.

The guide as listener and watcher

Talk is definitely a part of every writing workshop. Sometimes meetings between classmates are planned for a discussion of a specific piece of writing. More often, casual talk just happens naturally as writers think out loud. So I eavesdrop a lot.

Someone will ask someone else how to spell a word. I listen to find out whether the answer is accurate (and often place a dictionary within arm's reach of the person asking). Or a writer is crumpling up the third piece of paper and trying for a two-point dunk into the recycling box. This is the time to talk about getting past writer's block.

"Quiet, Please. Writers at Work."

In writing workshops, there is time set aside for quiet, the kind of quiet that brings in chopped bits of conversation from people passing in the hallway or that lets us hear pens tapping dots on i's and periods at the ends of sentences. The kind of quiet that lets the writer think and imagine.

Negotiate with your classes the quiet time they want: when, how long, how often. During the silence, people may be reading or writing: both activities balance the workshop experience.

> I read a lot, mostly medieval stories. Reading helps me in that it brings out my own style of writing.
>
> The books that influenced me the most are probably the J.R. Tolkien series, also a couple of books by O.R. Melling called *The Singing Stone* and *The Druid's Tune*. Both these books helped me. It was like one big brainstorm page after page. Many ideas came to my head.
>
> SCOTT (GRADE 9)

> Read, read, read. Read everything — trash, classics, good and bad, and see how they do it. Just like a carpenter who works as an apprentice and studies the master. Read! You'll absorb it.
>
> WILLIAM FAULKNER

Writers who publish. . .

In a writing workshop, there will, of course, be those who will want to share their finished pieces. A bulletin board or a three-ring binder can serve as a "publishing" place for students who wish to display their work for others to read.

Our English department has a monthly publication, HOTTURNOVERS, where students may submit their poetry or prose for consideration by two of us teachers in the English department. Gold-coloured copies are presented personally to each HOTTURNOVERS writer by our principal — the one time students don't mind being summoned to the office!

Each year, we have our LITERARY FEAST. All writers who wish to display their work for others to read may do so; the only "rule" is that the writing must have been worked through revision to completion.

. . . and writers who don't publish

Many more students will write and not want to share their stuff at all. This doesn't mean that the workshops have failed — there's more to writing than publishing.

> Before, when someone died or was killed in my story that was it — they were dead and that was it, just plain dead. No strings attached, no feelings, and no tears. I have experienced a death, so now I can understand it better and get all of the feelings down on the paper.
>
> Writing sad stories helps me overcome bad feelings when I think about the death of someone who was very close to me. I'm also scared of death so I like to write stories about teens dying so I can try to understand how I would feel and go through it.
>
> CARRIE (GRADE 9)

I think I have said,
in most cases, what I have wanted to say.
And I don't think it's beautiful, nor is
beauty what I was after. I wanted to
find out — in my head and in my mind —
what I felt about things.

AL PURDY

CHAPTER 2

Freefalling into writing

Freefall is stacking lumber, mortar, and bricks from which to build.

W.O. MITCHELL

I learned about freefall in 1976 when I took the summer workshop sessions at the Banff School of Fine Arts, where W.O. Mitchell was the director of the writing course. Freefall seemed to me then (and now) to be a small miracle. Finally, my imagination opened up. Finally I sounded like myself.

Mitchell's analogy of freefall in writing to building supplies in constructing a house is helpful in explaining to students just how freefall works. It is that stack of lumber lying on the ground at the work site, waiting to be shaped. Neighbours aren't likely to come by, see that wood, and say, "Fine house ya got there." Freefall isn't shaped. It is the raw material of writing, a way of finding.

Why freefall works in the classroom

Students like freefall because it breaks all the writing rules. Forget about spelling. Let punctuation fall into place if it does, but don't search for it. If ideas bounce from one topic to another, then let them. When nonsense fills the page, keep pushing the pen forward. That's the freedom of freefall. It's play.

Getting started

I like to begin the writing course with a freefall workshop. First, students brainstorm for all the types of rules they know must be in a writer's mind when putting the finishing touches on a last draft. In minutes, the board is filled: grammar, spelling, punctuation, making sense, being neat, having interesting ideas, and more.

Then, I simply explain freefall by saying that it ignores all those rules. There is only one rule that must not be broken: Do not stop writing.

We're ready to begin.

"Trust me, it works!"

A five-minute timing is a good start in experimenting with freefall. Be sure everyone is settled with looseleaf and pen, and wait until the room is quiet. That will take a minute or so because some people will be in a small panic asking, "What'll I write?"

"Anything. Just start, and see what happens."

"But..."

"Think of what's been on your mind lately."

"I can't write about that."

"You can write about anything. You'll be the only one who reads this. Okay. Everyone ready now?"

"This is stupid. I don't know what to write."

"You haven't tried it yet. Maybe begin by writing 'I don't know what to write.' Just put down all the stuff your brain sends to you. Okay. Let's start now."

I always write with the class during the freefall time. Even if someone begins to whisper, I keep writing. When distracting sounds happen outside the room, they might become incorporated into the freefall for a few lines.

At the end of the timing, ask everyone to count the number of words they have written. To encourage all writers, I then ask students to raise their hands if they wrote more than twenty words (it is rare for anyone not to have achieved this). Then I raise the count to more than thirty, more than forty, and on until a only few people still have their hands raised.

There will be those who see the word count as a kind of competition, but I try to avoid that by reminding everyone about that single rule of freefall: Don't stop writing. Those with more words written have followed this rule more closely. They will explain to the class that they "just blocked everything out" or that they "wrote so fast my arm aches."

Developing freefall skills

Right away, do a second five-minute writing. Some students may want to continue the topic of the first one while others may want to begin something new.

When this second timing is finished, and the word count is done, ask how many writers have more words compared with the first time. Almost everyone will. They now begin to understand the connection between concentration and success in freefall.

The counting of words is not a practice that I carry into later timed freefall writing because the students easily get the point. Some individuals want to count each time, but that wears off after a while. Eventually, they just ignore the clock and write.

What is freefall for?

In this first workshop, it is important to get to the stage of looking back at the words that have been piling up on pages. Ask students to underline any ideas or phrases which they find interesting for whatever reason. If people find none, that isn't such a big deal because they have only written for ten minutes. Usually, though, everyone underlines something — many will read aloud to friends sitting nearby.

Because freefall is that lumber piling up, not yet shaped, do not ask that students read their freefall out loud to the class. Instead, invite people to tell what they were writing about. Perhaps start by talking about your own freefall to help the group get past the inevitable shyness of sharing writing. Even though quite a few people will not tell about their own writing, they all participate in this part of the workshop by listening to those who do share.

Freefall and writer's voice

This is an opportunity to begin to understand the concept of writer's voice and how it connects to freefall. What we write about is an important part of who we are as writers. Freefall gives us the themes that matter to us.

Also, because of the fast flow of freefall, we are less likely to be self-conscious about what we write and therefore less likely to hold back. Often, people who share their ideas will read a line or two directly from their freefall and we can hear those gems of success that are usually there even in a five-minute writing.

Following up on the first class

Over the next few weeks, continue to provide quiet class time for freefall and expect some to be done for homework too. The amount of time you give (or students take on their own) will vary, depending upon enthusiasm in the classes or upon your other curriculum responsibilities. It's my view that if we value something, we should take time out to do it, not simply talk about it. If we value the exploration of writing ideas, then we give time to do this together in class.

An easy way to identify freefall written outside class time is to ask students to put a colourful line under the work completed in class, then put the date and the time in the margin next to it. Visit each person and initial their line. It's a nice chance to make that personal contact with every student, complimenting, asking if they're interested in what they've written, encouraging those who may have only a few lines on the page.

When you do a homework check next class, it takes a simple glance to see whether more writing has been done below the colourful line. You'll easily learn who's enjoying freefall and has an idea cooking, who has little opportunity for quiet writing time at home, who needs a boost of self-confidence, and who just "forgot" to do the homework.

I don't actually read freefall because it isn't meant for a reader. It is the writer's chance to "find." Yet many students will read their freefall to friends or to me. Any comment I make is meant to encourage: "You're onto something here." or "I can see something beginning to take shape, can you?"

What does a writer do with freefall?

The shaping of freefall is much more complex than the first-stage writing of it. The following chapters of writing workshops will offer some insights into how students may develop their ideas. During this first writing month, though, brief conversations with writers can begin to help them move forward. I like to ask, "How do you see yourself using this writing? Is a story starting? A poem? An essay?"

If they can see the shape beginning, then it's time to put some of those writing rules back into place: make sense of ideas, cut repetition, develop themes, fix up some spelling and punctuation, and on and on.

Assessment in the freefall workshops

After about a month of experimenting with freefall, ask students to make a portfolio for assessment. They take one page of writing to revise to a finished draft. It is not a finished story, poem, or essay (although it can be). It is a sample of the "best page" of the month.

In terms of assessment, everything counts. Give classmarks for participating in the freefall workshops. Then, pile up more points for the early draft work as well as for the final draft of the "best page."

I provide each student with a file folder which they usually like to decorate and personalize. Into this folder they put the following:

- all pages of freefall organized by date and stapled together;
- the early draft(s) of their sample page of freefall organized by date and also stapled;
- the final draft of the sample freefall;
- the evaluation sheet.

There may be a few students who have some freefall which they do not want read by anyone, but they want them in their writing portfolio in order to get credits. I ask them to simply draw a diagonal line in pencil across those freefall pages as a signal that I must not read them. Or they could staple the page closed.

Key concepts in assessing writing

At our school, we've adopted the Vermont Assessment from Barry Lane's *After the End*. It is simple, complete, and works with any genre of writing. In addition to participation and thoroughness of revision, there are five basic assessment categories: purpose, content, organization, correctness, and effectiveness.

Before students rework their "best page" they can benefit from understanding each of these key concepts. Knowing how they will be evaluated helps students focus on the writing skills we are developing in the workshops.

Here are the simple questions which I use to help explain the assessment categories:

PURPOSE:	Who is your audience?
	What do you want your audience to know, think, or feel from reading your writing?
	Is your topic clear in the beginning?
	Did you stay on the topic?
CONTENT:	Did you say what you wanted to say?
	Are all your ideas clear?
ORGANIZATION:	Are your ideas presented in the best order?
	Is there a clear beginning, middle, and end?
CORRECTNESS:	Are spelling, grammar, and punctuation correct?
EFFECTIVENESS:	Is your writing interesting?
	Do you sound like you?

FREEFALL WORKSHOP EVALUATION

Name: __Tanya_____ Class: __11-3__
Date: __Feb. 18_____

1. Freefall Participation:
   a. Did I take part in the timed writings?
      (always) usually sometimes not yet
   b. Did I do the expected homework?
      always (usually) sometimes not yet

      My mark out of 10 is ___9___. *I can count always on you, Tanya!* ☺

2. Revising Freefall:
   a. Did I rework the ideas from my "best page"?
      (all) most some none yet
   b. Did I correct spelling and punctuation?
      (all) most some none yet

      My mark out of 10 is __10__. *yes!*

3. FINAL DRAFT OF SAMPLE FREEFALL:

1.	purpose	(A)	B	C	D	E
2.	content	A	(B)	C	D	E
3.	organization	(A)-(B)		C	D	E
4.	correctness	(A)-(B)		C	D	E
5.	effectiveness	(A)-(B)		C	D	E

      My mark out of 10 is __8.5__.

COMMENTS: *If I work on this some more I'll likely do better. But I ran out of time. I plan on working on this chapter. There's parts that don't sound right. Good writing takes time. I'm glad you're ready to "do the time." This story will be a "hit"! Mrs.*

With this sample "best page" of freefall, some of the evaluation categories must be loosely applied because of the nature of the assignment. For example, the one page may not have a "clear beginning, middle, and end" that a completed story or essay would, but the student can easily assess whether the ideas on the page are presented in the "best order."

Usually, when I give students an evaluation sheet, I ask them to self-evaluate. That gives me something concrete to respond to as I do my "teacher evaluation."

Celebrating writing success

When passing back these writing samples, bring attention to the successes by reading aloud from as many students' work as you can. Even to read one phrase or one line from each writer will help to celebrate all the voices in the class.

One classroom experience

There is a kind of magic in using freefall in the classroom because it does have so much success. But like all magic, it can be explained: freefall gives writers the freedom to do real writing. It doesn't seem like a school assignment because it develops from deep within each writer rather than from a text or from a teacher's specific plans.

One of my favourite experiences with using quiet writing time for freefall occurred during last period on a Friday afternoon.

I had my grade 10 class, many of whom weren't keen about school. So I gathered my own pen and paper and sat at one of their tables, waiting for them to stroll into the room.

Stephanie arrived first. "What're we doing? Writing?"

"Yea. I thought we'd do a bit."

Shaun was behind her. I had taught him also when he was in grade 8. "One of those five-minute things?"

"Yea. Or maybe ten."

Now the room was filling up and students were taking my cue, getting out their own supplies. Richard, who was repeating grade 10, came into the room last. "Oh no, not writing. It's last class."

"A nice, relaxing way to end the week, I thought."

He rolled his eyes.

Then Shaun said, "Remember when we were in grade 8 and we did double time?"

"Oh yea, I remember that." When the first ten-minute timing was up, we had started another. This second quiet period was used to continue writing or to reread what had just been done.

Richard took Shaun's comment as some kind of challenge. "Bet we could do twenty."

"Do I hear thirty?" I said and laughed.

But, to the class, this wasn't a joke. I could see it in the stack of looseleaf Richard borrowed from Sonia and in the way Scott shook his pen vigorously to get the ink flowing. Stephanie had already started.

"Well, let's give it a try," I said. "I'll tell you when fifteen minutes are up. If you want to keep going for another fifteen, do it. If not, read over what you have, or quietly rest. Ready?"

Everyone wrote. "That's fifteen," I said. No one stopped. So I put my own pen to page again.

"That's another fifteen."

I saw that Shaun was still writing; so was Joe. And Stephanie. And Sonia. Richard, like me, was casing the situation. When he started writing again, so did I.

During that next fifteen minutes, the students gradually stopped writing, but remained quiet.

"Forty-five minutes!" I said. "That's a record!"

"My arm's busted," said Richard.

"I wrote five pages."

"Can we tell about what we wrote?"

"Sure, we've got enough time to hear a few. Who wants to start?"

Last class Friday afternoon. I hardly believed it myself.

CHAPTER **3**

Guided fantasy

> My task which I am trying to achieve is, by the power of the written word to make you hear, to make you feel — it is before all, to make you see. That — and no more, and it is everything.
>
> JOSEPH CONRAD

This writing experience is one you might recognize from some of the stuff we did in the '70s. I used it then in my classes; I use it now. And I still get the same reactions:

"This is weird."

"Can we do this tomorrow?"

"That was so cool."

Some things just don't change.

What's a guided fantasy for?

To me, even if only a little writing happens, a guided fantasy is a fun way to relax. It's a break from the glare and strain of our busy lives at school.

In a writing program, a guided fantasy is a way to encourage students to explore their imaginations. It has been my experience that many people don't recognize that they have imaginations, let alone take time to actually explore the fantasy worlds there.

Getting started

To begin the mind journey, first, invite everyone to sit, slouch, or sprawl comfortably anywhere in the room. Turn out the lights. Then, set the "travelling" mood by guiding your students through a head-to-toe relaxation exercise.

It's important to wait for reasonable stillness — yet don't hush the giggles and groans too soon because everyone will feel a bit weird doing this at first. When things settle down enough, begin with a quiet voice.

First, just relax

"Before you begin your imaginary journey to a special place, I want you to be completely relaxed and comfortable. So you'll do some relaxing first.

"Tighten your toes. Curl them in tight and hold that tension. Feel as if your toes are glued together. *(pause)* Now relax your toes. Wiggle them around to loosen that tension you just had. Let them come unglued. Now, tighten your feet. Curl the bottoms of your feet and feel the stretch all along the top part. Hold that tension, but be careful not to make your feet cramp. *(pause)* Now relax your feet. Circle them around a bit so you can feel all the tension go away. Now, tighten your legs. Make them seem like wooden posts..."

Continue very slowly through the bottom, back, shoulders, arms, neck, head, and face. Encourage students to give up their whole weight to gravity, heaviness.

Warning: snoring may occur

Be aware that some students actually relax so much they fall asleep. Once, an over-tired boy even snored! It's best just to let sleeping students lie, as it were. Later, take a minute for a personal chat about planning for more nighttime sleep.

The guided fantasy

A SPECIAL PLACE

Think of a place, a special place where you choose to go because it's where you feel contented, or maybe where you feel excitement, or where there are wonderful memories of the past. *(pause)* Think of the emotions connected to your special place. *(pause)* This is where you'd like to visit again and again. *(pause)* Think about why you like being here so much. *(pause)* Look around you. There are so many familiar things. *(pause)* Glance around and notice as many details as you can. *(pause)* Is there something beside you? *(pause)* Is there something right in front of you? *(pause)* Walk around a bit so you can see as much as possible. *(pause)*

Now, take time to really look at one particular thing, a very special something which you have always associated with this place. *(pause)* What is it? Can you pick it up? Or is it something you stand beside to look at? *(pause)* Notice every detail. Shapes. Colours. *(pause)* What does it feel like? *(pause)* Take a deep breath. *(pause)* What are the smells here? *(pause)* They are so clear in your memory. Think about how these smells help to make this such a great place to be in. *(pause)*

Notice as much as you can. Look all around you. *(pause)* Look up. What do you see? *(pause)* How far away can you see? Look behind yourself. *(pause)* To the right. *(pause)* To the left. *(pause)* Maybe you are in a special room. Look out a window and notice the outdoors. *(pause)* What's the weather like? *(pause)* Do you see any people around you, or outside that window? Anything at all?

Take time to think about the best thing about this place, the quality that makes it so important to you. *(pause)* Is it special because of something you do here? *(pause)* or because of certain people? *(pause)* If you had to find one word to help someone else understand this special place, think of what that word would be. Just one single word. *(pause)*

Enjoy your place. *(pause)* Sit down somewhere and relax. *(pause)* Look around. *(pause)* Think for a while. Think of all the details of this place, the memories, the feeling you have here.

(The final pause should last as long as there is stillness, maybe for about a minute. Then you can bring the guided fantasy to an end.) When you are ready, open your eyes. Maybe stretch a bit. Please help to keep the room quiet by not talking yet. You'll get plenty of time to share experiences with your friends.

Jotting notes about the journey

At the end of the fantasy, allow a few silent minutes. You'll see when the "journey" mood changes in the room. Then, encourage students to write — get as much as they can on paper to recreate that place and that experience. This quiet writing time is, perhaps, five to ten minutes.

Usually, the students ask that the lights not be turned on. This works fine if you have windows to let in enough natural light. It sure does harshly change the mood when you switch those lights back on, so give a gentle warning.

Touching base with everyone

When the chatting starts, just stroll around eavesdropping on what people are saying to their friends, sometimes asking for reactions to the experience. Often, students will read their writing aloud to someone close by.

Follow-up

The next time the class meets, go back to the fantasy writing and ask students to take a minute to read over what they have written. Then, give a bit of quiet time for adding more.

Take the opportunity to have volunteers share their experiences by simply saying to the class what place they have visited during the guided fantasy. Some may even want to read parts of what they wrote.

Now, ask everyone to consider what they might use this writing for: is it the beginning of a poem? a setting for a story? a special place simply worth describing in writing? Perhaps use Joseph Conrad's words from the beginning of this chapter to begin a brief discussion of writer's purpose.

Then, take a few moments to touch base with each person in the room to find out what purpose they can see in their own writing.

Developing the ideas

As a home assignment, ask that two drafts of the students' poem, or setting, or description be completed. Give three or four days for this in order that there be enough "stewing time" for ideas to surface and grow. Also, if someone has writer's block, you will have time to help get the writing flowing.

Reader response and teacher evaluation

When the assignment is due, ask that students exchange with a friend who will read their piece and write a "reader response" to show how clearly they could see the place or feel the mood of it. I always require that people sign their name when they comment on another's work as a way of personalizing their response.

You might want to use a "reader response" sheet similar to the one which a friend designed for me to use (see next page).

When you collect these drafts for evaluation, it's helpful if you take time to write your own response as a second reaction to each piece. I mean this apart from the marking of the assignment.

Usually, I put my evaluation on a separate piece of paper which has the headings: purpose, organization, content, correctness, effectiveness, and comment. This comment includes the traditional teacher stuff, such as suggestions for help needed or compliments on technique.

For example, I read Mary's description of her grandparents' farm where she visits each summer and I responded as a reader: "This reminds me of a farm near Dollar Lake where we went every sum-

Response Reader Response Reader Response

Response Reader Response Reader Response Reader Response

_____
_____
_____
_____
_____
_____
_____
_____
_____
_____
_____
_____
_____
_____
_____
_____
_____
_____

Reader Response Reader Response Reader

mer when I was a kid. Oh, how I remember the smells of the barn, sweet and stale at the same time."

The comment on her evaluation sheet is from me, the teacher: "Nice variety of descriptive words, but some sound like the Thesaurus rather than like you. See me about voice, please."

Writing your own guided fantasy

You might enjoy writing a different guided fantasy for your students. I have two others which I've written. One is a train journey to meet someone special. The other one I call a "rock fantasy." I give each student a pebble which I collect in the cove in front of my house and they imagine exploring a two-storey version of their rock. This fantasy works so well that very few students want to part with their rock when the experience is over.

When you do create your own guided fantasy, just keep in mind that all the things you say have to be comfortable and safe. In the rock exploration, for example, I will say a couple of times that there is no chance that the students would fall because of the special connection they have with the rock. One girl described, later, how she climbed the steepest slope of the rock like a spider would!

One classroom experience with A Special Place

Mark wrote for about three minutes after the guided rock fantasy, and then he tossed his pen down. "This is all I can write."

When I asked him to jot a note to himself about why he stopped, he wrote: "Because I felt I couldn't complete the story without making it a dull ending. I couldn't be more descriptive of the place or voyage."

From this brief note, I could see that he was worried about being "dull." His final word "voyage" told me a lot: to Mark, this wasn't a static place, a mountain to look at — it was an experience, an adventure!

So I asked him to underline the first descriptive word in his paragraph. He chose "large."

"But I can't actually see that mountain, Mark. How large is it? What would it be like if I looked down?"

"The cars would be really small."

"Like what?"

"Ah...dinky toys."

"Write that down."

Then, I asked him to underline other places in his paragraph where he believed he could add more description. Soon, I was beginning to see his mountain more clearly.

I'm on top of a large sk. mountain in Feb'ry I look around and feels the coolness of the Breeze I see a river on north side by near an Extreme tall through the trees The river has many pools I see rocks covering the top with crystal white snow you can feel the coldness of the snow as I drop down a small cliff on my way down the trail with white powder Brushing Past your body you feel free to ski wherever you want to the mountain IS yours

large - like Being on top of the world. The cars at the Base of the mountain are dinky toys.
coolness - Frigid

north side - far Side of The mountain

Trees - Pine & Fir   Coldness -
                    drop - descend
Sess - wade   Brushing - Sprinkling
                                     Flowing
rocks - a granite rock   feel soft

Mark came for extra help a few days later and I saw that he had pushed description into his writing. It was overdone. I also noticed that he still needed to think quite a lot about some technical things: paragraphing, sentence length, capitalization, spelling.

But I could also see that he was feeling connected to this writing because he had given himself the pen name Nakiska, which is the name of that mountain run he was describing.

Home Mark went to give it another try. By the time the assignment was due, he had done a third and a fourth draft.

In the final draft (see previous page), I noticed that, around the name of the mountain, Mark had drawn four black diamonds, the symbols for a difficult ski run. And, though the pseudonym was still there, he had written his full name below it — Mark was growing in confidence, that was for sure.

When I asked students to jot themselves a final note about what they had learned in their draft work, Mark wrote: "To put feelings into the person that you are writing about. And to make their surroundings more mentally active to the reader. So they play on their minds."

There was lots more in that final draft that Mark could improve upon, I know. But it was only October. Lots of time for learning still left in our year.

CHAPTER 4

Composition connections

True wit is Nature to advantage dressed,
What oft was thought but ne'er so well expressed.

ALEXANDER POPE

An assignment on composition writing is usually met with about as much enthusiasm as exam timetables. Most students believe it's just not much fun.

Toss out topics

A key to all this gloom is that quite often the topics for those compositions are suggested by us teachers — they don't come out of the students' experiences. Remember being asked to write about what you had done on your summer vacation? I do. And even though I'd had a great time at Dollar Lake, tenting with my family and spending hot haying days on Sandy Dillman's nearby farm, I just couldn't get any of that fun to appear on the lines of my scribbler. I wasn't connected with that summer topic by the time September rolled around. Were you?

With that tedious experience in mind, I tossed out all my topic lists and looked for better methods to encourage students to find their own themes. This chapter suggests one way to do this successfully.

Reading begins the writing process

First, ask students to read articles from as many anthologies as you can collect for your classroom shelves. Individuals select six pieces of non-fiction to read and to "rate" on their own scale. A simple chart is used to keep track of this assignment. The purpose here is to begin the writing experience by reading the best that others have written. This may take a couple of class periods, as well as reading assigned as homework.

Rating Non fiction

Catherine
10 - 13

My rating code is.   great good o.k. poor awful

Anthology	Article	Author	Rating
1. Matters of fact	"The day Niagra Falls Ran dry."	David Phillips	good
2. Accelerate Destinations	"Lies my father told me"	Ted Allen	o.k.
3. Accelerate Destinations	"An attack on TV"	Jeffrey Schrank	great
4. " "	"Complaining"	S.C.A.C.A	good
5. " "	"Notes from Tibet"	Mark Abley	great
6. " "	"Logo Rhythms"	Kathleen M. Smith	poor

"And now for the best in the catagory of..."

As a way of encouraging students to reflect on their reading, have a kind of Governor General's Awards for non-fiction writing. Using the six articles read, students make their individual nominations for the "best" in these catagories:

- best title
- best opening sentence
- most interesting fact
- best closing sentence
- best overall article

Now, the students form groups of four or five and present their nominations. Each group's task is to arrive at a consensus for one choice in each catagory.

You will notice a lot as you eavesdrop on the discussions. Encourage people to explain their nominations with clear details. You might need to do a bit of refereeing, too, as enthusiasm turns to argument.

The decisions aren't important, here, really. It's the talking, the thinking. By the time each student has gone through this process, a lot of experience in non-fiction has been gained.

"What'll I write about?"

Now, it's time to move toward giving that composition assignment. But don't speak of word count, deadlines, or topics just yet. Wade in slowly.

I take classes to our library where there is a display of books of quotations. We have about eight of them, including *The Penguin Dictionary of Modern Humorous Quotations*, *Bartlett's Familiar Quotations*, and *Colombo's Canadian Quotations*.

Students browse through the collections to choose a quotation which they strongly believe in or find interesting in some way. Other books are available too, of course. A few students like to go directly to Shakespeare's plays, for example. Others check out quotations from current magazines or search through web sites.

Keeping the research simple

This research experience is an opportunity to teach students how to document sources. I ask them to list the bibliographic information in this order: author, book, place & publication, publisher, copyright year, and page. In the next workshop period, I take time to show exactly how to document sources. It's easy, then, for students to rewrite the bibliographic information in correct format using their library notes.

Picture this!

It may take a while until everyone has found a quotation, so it's best not to rush to the next step of this workshop. Go on with assignments on other aspects of the curriculum to give everyone time (perhaps three or four days) to select a quotation thoughtfully. Collect each research page to evaluate accuracy. I don't comment on the quotation itself because my ideas or interpretations might influence the student's thinking.

When everyone's ready, continue by asking for an illustration of the quotation, in original artwork, magazine cutouts, or computerized graphics. This activity is an opportunity for the writers to think more deeply about the ideas they've chosen. Lots of talk takes place around the cutting, gluing, thinking, and drawing.

As you stroll around the classroom watching the artists in action, you will have the chance to discover who hasn't quite understood the quotation they've chosen. These will be the students who stare blankly at their pages or who tell you firmly, "There's no way to show a picture of this." With a bit of conversation, ideas can be clarified.

Stewing time

Set a deadline for the completion of the quotation illustration so that students can take enough time at home to do their best job. Three or four days should be enough.

Words are windows

Just before the deadline date for the illustrated quotations, create a classroom display space entitled WORDS ARE WINDOWS. (I've borrowed this title idea from e. e. cummings.)

When completed assignments are submitted, mark them for accuracy, clarity, and creativity. Then, begin to fill the display space. This will compliment those who've met the deadline and encourage others to catch up. I don't put up ones that have errors. Instead, I return them for correction so that, by the time they're on display, they all have full value.

These quotation illustrations are really quite interesting reading!

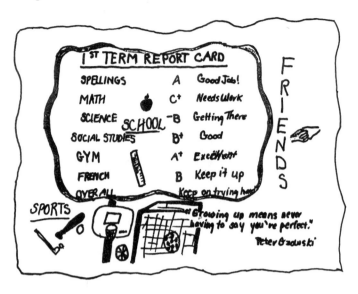

It's time to compose

It has been my experience that students become quite committed to the ideas in the quotation illustration by the time they're staring up at their own work on the WORDS ARE WINDOWS display. But I won't tell you that they jump up and down in delight when I set down the compositon requirements: word count, deadlines, revision expectations, etc.

Yet, they've been thinking of the issues and ideas in connection with this quotation for a few weeks now, so they are quite confident that they have something important to say. As they begin, remind them of how valuable talk can be in the writing process.

Guided conversations

Not all writers want to have conversations about their writing, but many do. You might want to display in your classroom the suggestions for peer talk throughout this compositon writing experience (see next two pages). They have been designed so that students can get feedback at various times in the process, either with a set of

MY TOPIC IS Living Life

WHAT WILL PEOPLE FIND
INTERESTING ABOUT MY TOPIC?

- The attitudes people have towards
life (positive or negative)
- what makes life fun.
- causes of depression, angry, hate.

INTRODUCTORY PARAGRAPH

**WHAT DO YOU THINK MY MAIN POINT
IS?** Love conqueing over hate.
If your willing to overcome
hate and move to the goodness
of some one you will find love.

**WHAT DO I NEED TO EXPLAIN MORE
CLEARLY?**
The first line is not explain,
all that clearly . Sentence
are to o wor dey and tooloms

REVISION

WHAT IMPROVEMENTS DO YOU NOTICE?

- more detail and descriptive words
- flows together better when added new sentences.
- happiness is expressed more than sadness.

HOW COULD I IMPROVE THE TITLE TO CREATE MORE INTEREST IN MY WRITING?

- Change the title to something new which is unique in its own way. Catch the readers attention with something to make them think more, about whats is going to be about.

PLEASE UNDERLINE ANY PROBLEMS YOU NOTICE IN SPELLING AND GRAMMAR.

PLEASE COMPLIMENT THE PLACES WHERE MY WRITING IS ESPECIALLY STRONG.

FIRST DRAFT

WHAT IDEAS ARE OUT OF ORDER?

None.

WHAT IDEAS ARE REPEATED?

more about downside of life then the happiness in life.

WHAT IDEAS AREN'T EXPLAINED CLEARLY?

- go into more detail on happiness

WHAT DID YOU FIND MOST INTERESTING?

Introduction, ending

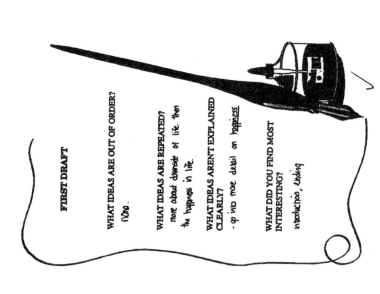

pre-determined questions or by creating questions specific to their own writing. Both work well.

When students are ready, they find a friend to chat with, using a small note-taking sheet to focus their conversation. It's important that the writer ask the questions and take the notes. This will keep the control in the owner's hands so that comments written down are only those which the writer has found important.

For students who don't like to have peer conversatons, these same note-taking sheets can be used to focus personal reflections.

Theo's experience

Theo was in my grade 10 class. He had transferred in about a week before this composition workshop began, announcing that he had a "learning disability."

"I can't write things down," he said.

In the library, he looked for quotations with not too much enthusiasm. But something was different — he wanted to talk. And talk. Not with his classmates and not off the topic. Theo wanted to talk about a quotation by Isaac Asimov. His ideas were well articulated and very interesting.

But he was right the first time: he sure did not write things down. Even Asimov's words didn't inspire Theo to put pen to page.

So when I asked students to begin the first drafts of their compositions, Theo turned down the invitation flat. He folded his arms. He stewed. I tried to encourage him. I failed.

When I was on the other side of the classroom helping another student, I heard Theo mutter, "Composition sucks."

"Great!" I said. "That's your topic, Theo. Write it down."

"Huh?"

"Composition sucks," I repeated. That got a few laughs from the class, of course. "I can tell that you feel really strongly about that so get writing."

Surprisingly, by the end of class, Theo had written a small paragraph. I suggested that he use a tape recorder at home to talk all his ideas out to a point where he could reflect back on them. Then transcribe. He did.

The result was a composition which became a favourite of the class. Writing as subversive activity, it would seem.

Here's Theo's closing paragraph:

> And what reward does Theo receive if he does these compositions, you ask? That's the kick in the chops. He looks forward to grades 11 and 12 asking for 800-word essays so he can have the honour of going to college or university to write an essay or a composition in every course he takes!

What I like most about Theo's grade 10 composition is the hopefulness in that last paragraph: even though he had a "learning disability," Theo knew he was on the way to grade 11 and then grade 12 and then further.

Slow things down to a thoughtful pace

At this point in the composition workshop, give quite a bit of class time for writing and conversation until you are confident that each writer has a clear direction. I find that everyone is fairly busy for at least two one-hour classes.

After that, give the option to continue the writing at home and to use class time for quiet reading or other independent activities. The students who are struggling with the composition will then have lots of time for help and encouragement from you.

Celebrate the writing with readers

When the compositions are completed, they're ready for readers. Here I'm not speaking of teacher evaluation — that comes later.

Use the "reader response" idea from the guided fantasy workshop. Ask each writer to share their composition with at least two other readers, and give class time for this to happen. For those who'd rather have family members or friends from other classes read their work, simply record that the work is completed on time and let them submit it for evaluation later.

40

This story is a real outlook on life. I feel that we should try hard to be happy and keep a smile on our faces. Sometimes you do feel sad, but keep telling yourself to think positive and be thankful for all the good things in life. Life is too short to be frowning, so live it up to the best and enjoy yourself. Put love in your heart and make lots of friends and you will enjoy every minute to its fullest. Keep smiling!

J. Nannie.

41

Writing is for reading

When you pass back the evaluated compositions, the process does not need to stop there. Our school has published whole pieces as well as excerpts in our monthly publication of student writing called HOTTURNOVERS. Maybe you'll want to create a class anthology. There could be a library display for students in other classes to enjoy. Local medical offices may want to offer some of these compositions next to the *Readers' Digest* from 1976 and the illustrated explanations of how the human digestive tract works.

This year I'm going to decorate a box and take some compositions to a seniors' complex near our high school. Maybe some students will come with me and read their compositions aloud.

Meanwhile, in your writing course, lots of marks will have piled up for the students: class participation, researching, illustrating, draft work, revision, reflecting with or without peer conversation, final draft work, and sharing with readers.

What a lot of work! What a lot of thinking! And possibly a bit of fun, too!

CHAPTER 5

Finding character in fiction

Daydreaming had started me on the way, but story writing,
once I was truly in its grip, took me and shook me awake.

EUDORA WELTY

Creating character is a fun way to begin any fiction writing. There,
inside your head, is a living, talking, walking character — who
knows what can happen next?

But where do writers get their characters? How do they shape
them so convincingly on the page as to make us believe they must
exist?

First steps in creating character

To one student, a blank page can hold the excitement of beginning a
new journey, while to another it can simply be intimidating. For
both these types of students, it's best to get words moving onto the
page quickly so they can see characters emerge.

Start by asking students to make quick-note answers to these
questions which you ask aloud:

1. Is your character male or female?
2. Is your character tall? average height? short?
3. Is your character average weight? underweight? overweight?
4. What colour hair does your character have?

5. Think more about hair now. Is it long, short, medium length? Is there any particular style that you notice?
6. Look into your character's eyes. What colour are they?
7. What clothes would your character typically wear? Any favourite colour or style?
8. Now, picture that you are in a very crowded place (a mall, perhaps, or a school dance). You are trying to find your character. Is there anything that would make him/her stand out in a crowd?
9. Where does your character live? In the city? the suburbs? the country?

   • It's worth mentioning, here, that writers have to know the place they choose to write about. If students want to make Hawaii their setting, they'll need to be willing to do some research if they haven't been there.

10. Look at the place where your character lives. Is it a house? An apartment building? A house-trailer? What type of dwelling does he/she live in?
11. Now, notice the environment around this dwelling. Is it luxurious? Needing upkeep? What do you see around this place?
12. Does your character have a name yet?

   • The telephone book is a great resource for names.

13. Think again about where your character lives. Does anyone else live there? a friend? parent or parents? children? pets?

Tension in fiction

Now, it's time to go further into the fiction. Ask everyone to draw a line under the list of characteristics they have decided upon.

Because no story can develop without a problem, each writer needs to make decisions about conflict. Something's got to be going wrong in some way or there will be no tension, no reason for a reader to turn the page.

It may take a bit of thinking time and some discussion for students to come up with a problem. Encourage them to look back over their list of characteristics and see if there's any hint of what might create tension.

What if...

Now, ask students to draw another line, this time under the problem they have created.

All writers daydream. And the two words that often begin the daydreaming are: *What if...*

Ask everyone to write those two words, then give time for them to stop and daydream about what might happen to their character who has a particular problem.

Again, this will take a bit of time. Usually, though, everyone will have a sense of "What if" before the period ends. I don't give suggestions to those who are stuck because the story isn't mine. Instead, I read aloud a few characteristics from their list, and read their problem. Then I say, "Well, what if...?" Usually, this moves the thinking forward.

Keep reassuring the writers that all decisions can be changed, revised, cut. We're just in the beginning stages so far.

When it looks like everyone has a "what if," invite them to write for five minutes as a way of thinking. Reassure them that this freefall is *not* intended to be read by anyone else. They may want to begin with *dialogue* by having their character say something to someone, or they may want to begin by *describing* a place or an object or an event which is important to the character.

When the five-minute timing is finished, some writers will want to share what they've done. They could tell a bit about what has been written, or read some aloud. I often tell about mine first, just to get things going.

Giving characters a chance to grow

Now, it's time to give time. Ideas need to bubble and percolate in the mind's secret corners. Ask students to do a minimum of one hour's writing at home over four to six days. They could choose to do fifteen minutes a day, or longer chunks of time — whatever works for them.

Making connections with each writer

On the day the homework is due, the following questions can be used as a quick connection between you and each of the writers in your class:

1. How much time did you write?
2. Was your writing time successful? Explain.
3. Do you plan to develop this story idea? Explain.
4. Do you need any teacher help at this point? Explain.
5. Give yourself a mark out of 10 for this fiction homework. Explain why you deserve this mark.

I find this homework survey useful and interesting reading. These comments from some of my students reveal a lot about their learning:

You really do not realize how much you write is about your life until you experience it for yourself!!

MATTHEW (GRADE 12)

My problem is that I have really, really good ideas in my head and I'm excited to get them down on paper. So I start writing and within minutes I hate what I have written because it comes out all wrong and to me looks childish and corny. I immediately stop writing and have a bad attitude.

JESSE (GRADE 12)

Writing this story is fun. It is totally individual and lets you be yourself and think about what you are interested in and enjoy.

VIDA (GRADE 11)

Follow-up

To continue this fiction workshop over the next few weeks, try some in-class writing as well as more home assignments. The goal is to move the fiction forward — start to develop the character and the plot.

Here are some quick five- to ten-minute timing ideas which are designed to help writers get to know their characters better. In each writing class, I present one of them as a possibility. It is very important that these be suggestions, not requirements. Some writers will already have their fiction "cooking" and will not need any help in getting deeper inside the story.

- Write a letter as if your character were doing the writing. Who would they want to send a letter to? Why? Or, maybe your character has just received this letter from someone else in the story. Who would it be? Why would they be writing to your character?
- Take your character to a place where he/she is all alone. Where is that place? Why is your character there? What is he/she thinking about?
- Imagine your character picking up an object. What is it? Describe every detail. Why is this object important to your character?

It usually isn't long before the students will not need writing suggestions — the fiction moves itself along.

Assessment of unfinished fiction

Evaluating does not have to be done only when a short story is completed. Some students in your class may have the beginnings of novels, too. A sample scene submitted by each writer can be enough to use in end-of-workshop assessment.

Once students have handed in their writing folders, use the basic ideas that were described in the first workshop, "Freefalling into Writing." Credit is given for participation, revision, and final draft.

Celebrating writing success

When you return the writing folders, there usually will be some students who want to read aloud their polished scenes to the class. You might get things started by offering to read some, if the writers are a bit shy.

One classroom experience

Wendy was in grade 9. She had created a character close to her own age and had given this fictional girl a very serious problem: she regularly babysits in a nearby subdivision and, when the father of the family drives her home late at night, he assaults her.

As Wendy worked through the beginning stages of this story, she was tentative. "Am I allowed to write about this?"

"Do you think it's an important issue?"

"Yes."

"Then, write it."

Wendy's character was unlike Wendy, it seemed. Her silky long hair contrasted with Wendy's unruly blond curls. Her slim gracefulness was the antithesis of Wendy's thin, gangly body. But, eventually, I would learn that the serious issue which her character was dealing with had been Wendy's own nightmare.

Where else does fiction come from than the edges of our own experiences? If, as teachers, we're going to offer writing workshops that find meaning "beneath the ink," then there will be times we have to get involved in the consequences of that depth.

The first time Wendy actually asked me to read her fiction, she had created dialogue which took place in a car when the babysitter was being driven home. I had known Wendy since she'd been in my grade 7 class: laughing, loud, crazy Wendy. This dialogue had none of the zaniness I would have expected in her writer's voice; yet it was gripping, frightening.

Then one day Wendy asked me: "Is this too gross?"

I almost phoned her at home that night, so convinced was I that this wasn't fiction. The next morning, I saw Wendy with her usual clutch of friends and I waved for her to come to see me.

"I'm worried about you," I said.

"Yea, well, I thought you'd be. It's not happening now. No way. I don't babysit there anymore."

This news was such a relief! "But, what about the next babysitter?" I asked. "And the next?"

For a short while, her fiction was put aside. Wendy and I talked a lot. She didn't know that I was legally obligated to reveal what I knew, but I could see that she was almost ready to make the courageous step herself. And she did.

The fiction did get finished eventually. Wendy had her character phone the wife of the man who had assaulted her. That intense phone call pushed the fictional woman to believe the worst. I could see in that dialogue all the words Wendy had wished she herself had spoken two years ago. Catharsis.

And in real life? Wendy pressed charges.

One day late in June when I took the yearbook staff out for a quick supper, Wendy grabbed my hand and dragged me outside the restaurant.

"There he is! It's him! Quick, look! In that blue truck!"

I didn't get a chance to actually see the man. He'd seen Wendy first and he was getting out of there fast. He was afraid of her! And she wasn't afraid of him anymore.

He served a jail term. More babysitters than Wendy had the opportunity to tell their stories. Some things in life (and in fiction) work out the way we want them to.

If we're going to ask our students to explore characterization and motivation, we have to remind ourselves that fiction begins in the soul of the writer. Each time we read their words, we are taken close to that inner world. That proximity deserves our thoughtfulness and our respect.

CHAPTER 6

Keeping the writing going

It will come in its own time if it is meant to be so. Of course, it won't come without my help.

MARGARET LAURENCE

Okay, so we've got characters and we've got some fiction started. But how can students be encouraged to keep the writing going?

Looking at story structure

Teenagers have had lots of experience reading stories, either in school or at home. So I find that it takes a simple review of story structure to remind them of how they need to shape their own fiction.

What better way to look at a whole story than with a picture book for young children? It's easy. It's short and complete. And it's a bit of silly fun.

I have one of Nancy Wilcox-Richard's Farmer Joe "big books": *Farmer Joe's Hot Day*. This is a story about a farmer who complains to his wife that the day is so hot, he can't work. Her advice to him is to put on layers of clothing: hat, scarf, coat, mittens. Finally, the farmer gets the point and removes those excess layers, deciding never to complain again. Nancy lives close to our school (we have the same postal code!), so using her work is a way of celebrating a neighbour.

Before I begin to read Nancy's story, I ask students to brainstorm about what ingredients every story needs. Although they may not always come up with the specific literary terms, they do know what makes a story complete: characters, problems, setting, plot, climax, ending — these things have been "drilled" into their minds more than once, I'm sure.

To keep the lesson light, I ask students to settle in comfortably and imagine themselves as six-year-olds. As I read (or there may be a student who'd like to do the reading), everyone is thinking about how Nancy shaped her story of Farmer Joe: who were the characters? what was Farmer Joe's problem? and so on.

Visualizing the story curve

When the reading is finished, I ask students to form small groups to discuss the story structure and to draw it in the traditional curve. On the curve, they can plot the introduction of the problem, the rising action with its complications, and on to the climax and conclusion. It's all there, simply.

Making connections

The transition from a group discussion of Nancy's Farmer Joe book to individuals considering the structure of their own fiction is easy. Some writers will be into their stories enough to actually see the whole curve. But others need not feel discouraged if they are still exploring the character and events — this curve concept will be there in the back of their minds as they continue to write.

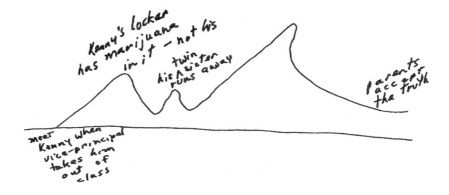

Scribble, cut, add, revise

It can feel as if the writing is failing when ideas created last week now seem weak or when whole scenes just don't seem logical anymore. New writers have been fooled (by the skillful craft of published authors) into believing that writing is simple. It was Eli Mandel, at a writing workshop in Banff, who first gave me the security of knowing that "All art is the art of hiding the art." I could relax, knowing that the struggles I was having with my writing would, eventually, be smooth surfaces my readers would glide over.

Seeing is believing

I take the stack of rough drafts from one of my earlier novels to school, and pass the chapters around. Students find a "messy" page and count the number of changes I made (27, 34, 49...).

Then I wait (because I know it will happen) for someone to say, "Gee, you make a lot of mistakes."

Cue the teacher for the important lesson: "Improvements," I say. "Not mistakes. These are all the places I reconsidered and saw better ways to write. I'm actually quite proud that I thought so hard."

It works. People loosen up about revision, they begin to see the potential for success in their scribbles.

Maybe you have your own novel in the bottom drawer of your desk at home, or you've recently written a business letter, or an article for a professional journal, or some poetry, or an outline for lesson plans. Whatever you have that you can share would be a worthwhile encouragement to your students: all writers make a mess.

I'm wondering. . .

When the fiction has some structure to it, ask students to attach a comment sheet upon which they have written two or three specific questions about their rough draft writing. That way, you will know exactly what each writer wants to learn about — you have a place to begin. Here are some questions students have recently asked in the "I'm wondering" assignment:

* What do you think of how I switch scenes from the father upstairs reading the diary to the downstairs scene where the daughter is on the phone?

MICHELLE (GRADE 9)

* Do you think it's believable that the twins would meet like that so long after they were separated?

SARA (GRADE 11)

* Does my title make you want to read the story?

KARL (GRADE 12)

* With just this scene, does it make you curious about the rest?

BROCK (GRADE 10)

As long as students see your comments as one reader's ideas and not "the answer," your responses to their questions will help them to continue thinking. They can also have a classmate answer the same questions, if they want more than one view.

Ending without stopping

It takes a long time to write a story successfully. Some students will work over several weeks or even more than one school term. Lindsey, in my grade 12 class this year, completed a short story which she had started in grade 9! But there are ways in which we can celebrate the writing without waiting for completed pieces. This chance for sharing can also help to encourage writers to keep going.

Assign each student to complete three to five pages of their story. This includes attention to spelling and grammar, besides the jobs of pulling the reader into the story and of creating believable characters and situations. If a title has not yet been decided upon, a working title can be used.

Then, use the "reader response" process (by now students are quite used to this) before you make your teacher evaluation.

Here is a comment which one grade 11 student received on his "reader response" sheet:

Ted, I liked your story, or at least the part I read. I like your descriptiveness and carefulness to expression of detail. Is the main characters' name Latale or Latalē? The story flows very nicely and gels together. I give it 2 thumbs up.

Eddy

It isn't always easy to convince students to do revision. "I don't do drafts" is often a comment made by inexperienced writers. So, I require that students reflect on their writing when it has been evaluated and returned. This may be done at any time throughout the term, or at the end of a term.

REFLECTING ON WRITING

PART A: Reworking/Revising

Find a place in your rough draft writing where you had made significant changes (*look for a mess!*).

1. Re-write the words as they had originally appeared in the rough draft.
2. Re-write the words as they appeared in the final draft.
3. Explain clearly why you made the change(s). Be specific and thorough.

PART B: Proofreading (grammar)

Find a grammar error which you made on your final draft.

1. Write this grammatical error.
2. Then, revise to solve the problem.

PART C: Proofreading (spelling)

Find FIVE spelling mistakes you had made in your writing this term. (If you have fewer than five errors, congrats!)

1. For each mistake, write the word wrong and then correct the mistake.
2. Look for any patterns in the mistakes you have made. Write a brief note to explain one of these spelling-error patterns.

PART D: Best Writing

Choose a sample of your best writing from this experiment in fiction and rewrite it. Then, explain clearly why you believe this to be your best writing.

The writing habit

Today is a holiday from school, and it's ten to eleven in the morning. I'd be in my second class of the day, probably asking Melissa to stop tilting her chair backwards as she reads her novel or reminding Richard that he hasn't yet passed in his vocabulary development assignment yet. Maybe Kyle would have finished the autographed copy of Kevin Major's *Far from Shore* and he'd be asking to borrow Diane Wieler's *Bad Boy* because it's autographed too.

For sure I wouldn't be inside my own head working out these words which are tumbling across the screen in front of me now. I have the writing habit, using weekends and holidays to push myself towards completed books.

Some of our students have that same habit. But it's more likely that the majority of them prefer talking to friends on the phone, or playing sports, or watching TV. So when this series of fiction workshops is finished, most students will stop there. I don't see that as a failure at all. They've played with fiction; their experiences are widened.

And I know that those addicted writers have had an opportunity to learn how to continue.

CHAPTER 7

Viewpoints

Time will change and even reverse many of your present opinions.

PLATO

If there's one thing teens like to do in school, it's chat with their friends. What do they talk about? What did we talk about when we were teens? Fashions, habits, trends, likes, dislikes, other friends — the list could wrap itself around the school. So it makes sense in a writing workshop to tap this resource.

Getting nosy

"Viewpoints" is a writing workshop based on students conducting surveys or interviews. They can satisfy that need to talk — then bring back information to use as the foundation for an opinion essay.

When I announce that they will be given permission to leave the classroom so they can ask questions to people in our school, the energy is up. They want to charge out of the room right away.

Formulating the questions

Ask your students to decide upon an important issue which would interest many people in the school. Easily they will come up with lots of ideas: fads, fashions, school rules, habits, music, TV shows, and so on.

Some will want to work alone and others in pairs on this "viewpoints" assignment. It doesn't work that well with more than two on the team because, when it gets to the writing stage, it can get a bit complicated sharing the tasks.

Once the topic has been decided upon, ten questions are formulated. The first few questions seem to hit the page in a flash, but then things slow down. You'll find that a bit of conversation with each team or student can draw more ideas out as they think more deeply about their topic. Usually this takes about one class period.

Organizing and expanding questions

When the ten questions are drafted, encourage everyone to rethink each question: is it clearly worded? should it require an explanation or example? when should one question be asked in relation to the others?

This organizing time not only helps the students to plan their interviews and surveys, but it also gives them the opportunity to think of their own responses to their questions. Already, they're formulating the concepts they'll write about later.

Still more decisions to make

When the ten questions are finally ready, the students will need to decide just how they want to proceed. Some may want to make copies of the questions to hand out. There is also the option of creating an answer grid for simple recording of ideas when people are surveyed orally. A one-on-one interview is another method which can be used to gather information if people prefer an in-depth talk with just one person.

Let 'em loose

For about three or four days in a row, students can "book out" of the classroom to do their surveys and interviews. To avoid chaos, it is best to have three to five teams or individuals out of the room at the same time. I give them twenty-minute blocks of time so that they can gather some information, then return to class to begin to organize their ideas. Later, they can "book out" again.

From specific to general

When all the facts and opinions are gathered, students will want some guidance as they look at all these details and try to create some general statements to use in their writing. Review the graphing concepts they've likely learned in math classes (pie graphs and bar graphs seem to be easiest).

The calculators will be out and pencils will be busy as students compile their statistics: how many people thought this or that? of these, how many were male? female? in grade 10? grade 11? grade 12? Depending on the issue they're exploring, the categories will, of course, vary.

It will take two or three classes (perhaps with homework time as well) for all the statistics to be compiled.

Magazine articles as models

Our national news magazines often use opinion polls or statistical surveys to back up the information in their articles. Find current issues in some of these publications to use as models.

In small groups, students can read the articles to see the connections between the graphs and the information given in the printed text. Ask the groups to list the things they notice which make the ideas in the magazine article clear and interesting. Then, one person from each group can report these findings to the class.

Making connections — making plans

Following the group investigation of the magazine models, ask individuals to write a note that describes how they will design their own essays: what details from the surveys or interviews will be focused on in the essay? which information will be shown in graphs? what form of graphs will they use? what will be written under the graphs?

At this point, it can be helpful to the students if they submit their work so that you can evaluate and offer suggestions. They can organize their written work in a folder, stapling surveys or interviews separate from their planning notes. If students are working in pairs, they share one folder.

Revisit the composition workshops

This writing assignment seems to get easier from this point on because the students already have experiences to draw on from the composition writing workshops. Ask them to dig out those thought webs and rough drafts, etc. from a few months ago. Remind them of the usefulness of the peer-conference sheets.

As a way of focusing on skill development, each student could write a note describing one skill they used well in that composition experience, and one which they will be improving upon. Through that note, you will see opportunities to give individual instruction as this workshop continues on to completion.

One classroom experience

Mark was repeating grade 10 and it looked as if he might repeat again, or drop out of school. Krissy was a neighbourhood friend of his, more like a younger sister, and she was now in his class.

Attendance wasn't a priority for either of them, but Krissy at least attempted to catch up on assignments missed. I pulled both of them through these writing workshops as if their feet were in quicksand.

Addicted!

The day I introduced this "viewpoints" writing experience, both Mark and Krissy seemed zapped with interest. Two factors contributed to this: they were addicted to smoking and they were to be given a chance to leave the classroom together. In seconds, they knew that tobacco was to be the focus of their writing and they would be able to trek on out to the school's restricted smoking area to question other addicts.

It wasn't an easy task to encourage them to do a top-quality job of creating their questions and of reflecting on the magazine models. They wanted out! And, for once, it wouldn't be called "skipping"!

Lies and truths

Finally, Krissy and Mark were ready to head out to the smoking area with their survey questions and their answer grids.

"Remember, you two, you're journalists," I said. "This means you're not out there to smoke. You're out there to gather information."

"Right," said Mark.

"Yea, right," said Krissy.

Sure, Gunnery, I said to myself. And elephants will fly.

They returned a bit red-faced (it was, after all, February in Nova Scotia) and proud of all the details about tobacco addiction they'd gathered: when people started smoking, how much they smoked, whether their parents knew, whether smokers thought cigarettes were too expensive, whether they thought of quitting, and more.

When I sat with them to hear how things went, the old and cold fumes of cigarette smoke hung in the air around the two of them. "Did you journalists manage not to smoke out there on assignment?"

"Sure, sure," said Mark. But he wasn't looking at me.

"Smells a bit like an ashtray here at your table."

"Yea, well," said Mark quickly, "they were all smoking, right? So we got the second-hand stuff. Couldn't help it. It's all over our clothes." He kept his jaw-bone stiff so he wouldn't give away that urge to grin through the lie.

"Look, Ms. Gunnery," said Krissy. "I'm not gonna lie. We smoked."

At this point, Mark's jaw dropped. He figured she was setting them up for yet another detention from the vice-principal.

But Krissy continued, "You don't expect us to go out there and look like a couple of nerds not smoking with all our friends puffing

SMOKING SURVEY

by Mark and Krissy

TOPIC: What we think about smoking

PROCESS: We plan on asking 50 people these questions and we'll keep a chart of what they say.

1. Do you smoke?

    never ❑   sometimes ❑   usually ❑   always ❑

2. How old are you?

    under 16 ❑   16-18 ❑   over 18 ❑

3. When did you start smoking?

    under 16 ❑   10-13 ❑   13-16 ❑   over 16 ❑

4. How much do you smoke every day?

    one or two ❑   about five ❑   more than five ❑

5. Do your parents know that you smoke?

    yes ❑   no ❑

6. Do your parents (or one of them) smoke?

    no ❑   sometimes ❑   a lot ❑

7. Do your friends smoke?

    none ❑   a few ❑   most of them ❑

8. Why do you smoke?

    addicted ❑   like the taste ❑   my friends do ❑   other?

9. Do you think cigarettes are too expensive?

    not really ❑   a bit expensive ❑   very expensive ❑

10. Do you think there should be taxes on cigarettes?

    none ❑   lower taxes ❑   the same ❑   higher taxes ❑

11. Do the warnings on packages make any difference to you (like do they make you think you want to quit)?

    none ❑   a bit ❑   quite a bit   a lot ❑

Thank you for your time.

away like chimneys. What kind of answers would we get from them if we did that? None, that's what. Now, I'm not saying we had to smoke, but that's the way we saw it."

Mark started to relax. Krissy was sounding pretty good. Maybe she was actually right about why they'd had a cigarette while they were out on assignment.

"I see your point," I said. I confess to being a bit of a pushover. "I've read about journalists who risked their lives pretending to be members of street gangs so they could get the inside story. Maybe I should be giving you bonus points for on-the-job risk to your lungs."

Addicted to success

Mark and Krissy continued through the process of this writing workshop with more comfort and interest than I had seen all year. When the final draft of their article, "Up in Smoke," was completed, both of them were obviously proud of it. Although they didn't want to read it to the class, they gave me their permission to read it aloud while they both leaned back in their chairs, listening, soaking up the accomplishment.

CHAPTER 8

Poetry

Poetry is emotion recollected in tranquility.

WILLIAM WORDSWORTH

Poetry is concise. Every word, every blank space, every dot on the page has meaning.

Many students are reluctant to give that extra time needed to get inside the meaning of poetry. One of my grade 12 students, Kathy, said to me the other day that poetry is too hard in high school. "The la la la rhyming stuff used to be easy," she said. "But this stuff's weird. Like I read a poem and my mind's blank."

Reading begins the writing process

It's my strong belief that all Kathy needs is experience with poetry. When students seem to be as "stuck" as she is, maybe they just need to team up with someone else to read and talk together.

I like to use the same rating process as we used with the non-fiction writing:

- Individuals read 10 poems and rate them.
- Decisions are made for "best" in several catagories: title, theme, line, image, style, and whole poem.
- Small groups meet so that individuals may present their nominations.
- Groups arrive at a consensus for the "best" in each catagory.

What's poetic?

To encourage more thinking and talking about poetry, invite students to look back over their reading lists and select one poem which was particularly interesting. Then ask them to choose one or two lines which they would describe as especially poetic.

These poetic samples make a colourful classroom display, rewritten on plain paper and illustrated with drawings or magazine pictures.

Talking is a writing activity

From this display, there can be whole-class discussion about what "poetic" actually means. Make notes of what they say on the board, a flip-chart, or an overhead during this discussion. As ideas are presented by the students, time can be taken to teach the more technical words (imagery, symbolism, interior rhyme, etc.) when students do not know them.

How is an iceberg like a poem?

Share with the class a poem which has quite a bit of complexity. I especially like e.e. cummings for this because it takes students a while to begin to see the layers of his thinking. For example, this poem looks like nonsense until the reader takes time to notice what's happening with the shape of the poem:

I

I(a

le
af
fa

ll

s)
one
l

iness

Below the surface of this poem is a depth of meaning much in the same way as below the surface of the ocean an iceberg has much more depth that is not first seen.

Where does poetry come from?

I can still hear my grade five teacher while we were working on the human anatomy, 'Do a cinquain on human hearts.' We had to write it on a drawing of a real human heart, which we coloured:

Heart
Mighty, powerful
Beats slow and fast
Love your human heart
Life

That's not what writing is. Writing is working on something you wish to do, the topic you want to talk about. Before, when I wasn't able to write what I wanted in school, I worked at home and no one ever read it or saw it.

LANA (GRADE 9)

Playing with words and images

This activity is an easy starter, especially for those reluctant poets. First, talk about the differences between our conscious minds and the subconscious. Once these two concepts are clear, we're ready to begin this activity of letting our subconscious "find" a poem.

Finding poetry

Distribute a few magazines to all the students. They also need pens and looseleaf. Then, ask for quiet in the room as everyone tries to clear their brains of all thoughts so they can begin with a "blank" mind.

As people flip casually through the magazines, some words, or phrases, or images will seem to say, "Stop here." It is as though the subconscious mind is at work tossing up ideas into the conscious level. Without judgement, it is important to simply write the word, phrase, or image down to create a list of about a dozen items.

Taking a thoughtful look

Now, it's time to get the conscious part of the brain back to work. Students read their own lists and look for threads of connection which are inevitably there. They can cross out lines, rearrange words, add in new ideas.

Before too much time goes by, ask them to write a second draft, incorporating all the scribbles they've made on the original list of "found" ideas. If some are not feeling successful, give them a new stack of magazines so they can try again.

At this second draft stage, I ask if anyone feels as if they've got a poem beginning to take shape. Some will. I collect a few of these and read them aloud, asking the class to listen for images and themes beginning to hang together to create a whole poem.

Poetry is not accidental

I probably repeat the idea of "beginning" and "early draft" quite a bit more than is needed in this workshop. Of course, I want students to have fun with this finding activity; but, at the same time, I do not want them to see poetry as accidental.

This is a positive start to a poetry workshop because everyone can have success to some point. Many of these "found poems" are not taken through the process to a final, publishable poem. But that's okay. We've played with words. We've thought about the connections, themes, and order of lines. We've heard some poetry out loud, and we've heard some stuff that is clearly unpoetic.

We're on the way to more meaningful poetry.

"Emotion recollected in tranquility"

It was George Elliott Clarke, a writer from Nova Scotia, who reminded me so clearly of the courage of poets. In a weekend workshop, he asked all of us to think of an emotion we had had but kept to ourselves. Then we were asked to write about it for five minutes. Next, he asked that we read this out loud — every one of us. That wasn't easy. Finally, George asked us to choose bits and pieces from the freefall to shape a poem.

What I learned that day from George's workshop was that I should not expect that all students will have the bravery to pen their souls onto the page. But they can have some private time in class to give it a try, in a safe environment.

Because teenagers have such elastic and volatile emotions usually, perhaps we do not need to ask them to write about an emotion they've kept to themselves. Many will, of course; but we can begin by asking them to recall an emotional time which they see as important: joy, sadness, pride, disappointment, etc. The poetry that develops from this first freefall writing to a completed draft will be strong — "emotion reflected in tranquility."

One classroom experience

Maxine was in my grade 12 class. She was a pale young woman, struggling with a most horrific experience which had erased her childhood and pushed her into a fearful adulthood. Sexual abuse is, of course, one of those emotional secrets many young people keep to themselves.

But, thankfully, Maxine's counsellors and foster parents had supported her though the terror. Now, in our poetry workshop, she was ready to write. You already know the tension and the sadness we both felt together as she started to share her writing with me.

I will never forget how confident Maxine was the day she gave me one of her poems, copied carefully on blue paper and signed in her own clear signature. "I want this on the WORDS ARE WINDOWS display in the office," she said.

Here's her poem:

> Thunder and lightning
> Monsters and shadows
> You walking towards me
> Fear

It isn't always easy as our students share their innermost selves with us, but it's always worth it.

Giving time for process

Just as with the fiction workshop, in poetry writing, it's important to give time for the development of the poetry. So, once again, I require that a minimum total of one hour be spent drafting a poem over the next five days.

Reflecting on homework

When the homework is due, ask students to put all their draft work into their writing folders (careful organization is needed: drafts should be numbered and in order). Then, each person writes a note to reflect on this homework experience:

DEVELOPING POETRY

1. How much time did you spend on your draft work? How many drafts did you do?

2. Was your poetry writing successful? Explain.

3. Describe one significant change which was made between your first and last drafts. Explain why the change was important.

4. Is your poem finished? Explain why or why not.

5. Do you plan to continue with this poem? Why or why not?

6. Is there any help which you need at this time? Explain.

7. On a scale of 1 to 10, give yourself a mark for this homework assignment (*not* for the poem, but for the work you did to develop it). Explain why you deserve that mark.

** Note: Please submit your answers to these questions along with all the draft work on your poem.

Evaluation, Part I

When you evaluate these writing folders, it will not be drudgery. Each voice is different. Also, you do not have to read every word of every draft. The comment page tells so much, and it has encouraged the students to re-think their own poetic process.

As you read the poetry, concentrate on content and style at this stage. Indicate places where the poetry had meaning for you: a single word, a line, a whole stanza, perhaps the entire poem. Writers learn quite a bit from praise in the absence of criticism.

These notes which students wrote to me reveal a lot about the writer's process and insights:

I learned that poetry doesn't just "happen." It takes a lot of time and thought to get the final product.

RYAN (GRADE 11)

I'm trying hard not to put cliches in my poem. I invented a new word: bee-flowered day, instead of bright, sunny day.

RACHEL (GRADE 12)

In draft one, the words did not hold much meaning for me and it seemed as if I had heard that type of line many times before. It just didn't work. So I thought long and hard, first trying to change the words but keeping the idea so that there was more feeling. That was nice, but not good enough.

Then I decided to change the entire idea. It was a definite improvement, but still not what I wanted. So I began changing the wording in the new idea, and finally (after about an hour of work) I found my two lines:

Never crossing the gap between friends (draft 1)

The double-edged blade which hangs between friends (draft 4)

HILTZ (GRADE 12)

Getting to the surface

Once the writers are satisfied that the meaning of the poem is clear and complete (usually after about a week or so), you will find that the process will naturally evolve to the point where students are ready for proofreading, coming up out of the depths of creating ideas to the surface of the words.

Ask that they take a coloured pen or pencil and go through their writing first (they may want to ask a friend to proofread for them, instead). It is a lot less work for us teachers when students have already found the obvious errors in spelling and grammar or the places where their ideas are not clear.

Reader responses

Once again, the "reader response" sheets come in handy as a way of encouraging students to share their writing. Quite often, they're taken home to use with a family member or close friend.

From a younger sister: "The ending was unexpecting [sic]. I thought it was about losing someone. It was good because of the twist at the end."

From a best friend: "Your poem changed quite a bit from the first draft. When I read it, I saw pictures in my head."

From a classmate: "You write the coolest poetry. I really like the line 'For I am hate, Pandora's Box of the soul.' It's so cool and so true. Do you enjoy writing about evil and death and hate and fear? I bet it took a long time to write all 5 drafts of a 2 page long poem, didn't it?"

Evaluation, Part II

When the reader response is completed, it's time for teacher evaluating of the poetry. The same categories can be used for poetry as for other genres: purpose, organization, content, effectiveness, and correctness.

Celebrating Poetry

Provide a place in the classroom for finished poetry to be displayed — maybe a binder with a specially designed cover, or perhaps a decorated wall space.

Have a classroom coffeehouse where goodies are served and poets read their own work or the poems of their classmates. Maybe there's a guitarist who would accompany some writers, taking the time to rehearse before performing. It's the sound of the words, finally, that brings us closer to the poetry experience.

CHAPTER 9

Curtains up!

The play's the thing...

WILLIAM SHAKESPEARE

Some activities we do in class just don't seem like schoolwork to our students. Drama is one of these. It's play (pun intended).

Warming up

As a way of encouraging everyone to feel comfortable with performance, I like to begin with a theatre game. Each person writes on a small recipe card the following bits of information to help create a character:

> Character
> -name
> -sex
> -age
> -problem

All the recipe cards are tossed into a bag. (Keeping in mind that teens often like to stretch limits, I ask that nothing be written that would embarrass or offend.)

Then, to suggest the theatre mood, rearrange the class. Push tables and desks out of the way to create a "stage," and arrange the chairs into semi-circles for the audience. Chaos soon settles into expectation.

Volunteers form pairs or small groups: a mini-theatre troupe. One troupe at a time randomly selects a character card for each actor. Then the group is given two minutes outside the classroom to decide upon a situation in which to place these characters and to create a quick scene that will reveal all the information on the cards.

Although the group outside the class will always want more time, let them know that the "curtain's up!" The "stage lights" (simply the regular classroom lights) are turned off. In they come, set up a few chairs to represent seats on a bus, a kitchen table, a hotdog stand, or whatever. A student in charge of lighting flicks the light switch and the performance begins.

The task of the audience is to watch carefully to identify just who these characters are and what each individual "problem" is. When the performance is over, people in the audience tell the actors what they gleaned from their scene.

This activity is quick, focused, and a bit of fun. Most often the scenarios are zany, which the audience loves. I give two class credits during this warm-up activity: one for performance and one for taking part as audience. It's rare for students not to receive full credits.

Playwrights, pick up your pens

Now, students are warmed-up and ready to write short plays. Ask them to form theatre troupes of three or more people. With this activity, larger groups of even six can work well. Give them time to think of an original name for their troupe. This adds some team spirit.

Each troupe member now presents a character from his or her own short story (written a few months ago) as a possible character to use in their play.

Give discussion time for troupes to work out reasonable settings and themes into which all their characters can fit. I don't insist that they use their story characters, but it is a good starting point and many actually do work out well.

This pre-writing activity takes about one or two classes, with some troupes meeting at home or at noonhour in my class to work together.

Stage fright

Maybe the troupe has six members, but only four people want to act. We know that many teens are quite self-conscious about speaking in front of the class. So, as you listen to the early discussions, find out who seems keen and who seems quiet. A theatre troupe needs more members than the actors: directors, sound technicians, stage managers, etc. Reassure everyone that they can take part without feeling trapped in a job they don't like.

If "live" performance bothers everyone in the group, then they can design their script for radio or video. Puppetry can be another way for shy actors to "hide" from the audience. This script-writing workshop will go nowhere if the students begin by feeling terrified about how their script will be used.

Taking advice from Shakespeare

Before the ideas spill onto the pages, it's good to give students a chance to look at a published script as a model for their own writing. Some may not, for example, realize that dialogue in scripts does not require the use of quotation marks.

Since Shakespeare has earned the reputation of being the most famous of all playwrights, I like to bring him into the workshop to give us advice. We have class sets of many of his plays, so it's simple to have the theatre troupes glance through an act, noting patterns: how are acts divided? how do actors know when to speak? how are sounds, actions, and setting shown?

When the discussion slows down, begin by asking one troupe to present their findings to the whole class. Write these basic patterns of script-writing on an overhead or flip-chart. By the time each troupe has offered findings, students will have a complete list of reminders for how their scripts need to be written.

On the page, then on the stage

It will take three or four classes for each group to complete the first draft of their play. To make sure there's lots of time for stewing the ideas, spread out the writing classes rather than have them four or five days in a row. Again, some troupes will meet outside our class time.

Because a play is written to be in motion, it is not always easy for the writers to put all the noise and action on the flat surface of a page. Give a bit of time for workshopping the plays. Maybe there's an empty classroom so a troupe can "book out" of your room. Even a hallway space can be enough if the noise can be kept down (not quite an impossible task). Stairwells are good spaces for workshopping plays.

Soon, the drafts will have been tightened up and final scripts can be written. Throughout this writing workshop, it is a lighter marking load for us teachers because, in a class of thirty students, we are commenting on and evaluating perhaps five to seven scripts.

When the scripts are finished, I photocopy one for each troupe member, keeping one for myself as well. My copies later become part of a collection of all the original scripts displayed in a three-ring binder.

Coming soon to a theatre near you!

As the troupes are working through their draft work, take on the role of producer of all the plays. Make a calendar of production dates and have each troupe decide upon their own performance time.

Require that posters be designed for every play, colourfully representing the theme, announcing the production date, and listing the actors, directors, etc. These make a great hallway display and seem to add to the anticipation of production time. Sometimes, troupes will assign the poster task to one or two members only, or they may all co-operate to create it (rough design, lettering, drawing, colouring, cutting out magazine pictures, etc.).

In about a week or so, groups will be ready to perform.

"His hour upon the stage"

Those production days are hectic — one actor can't find his sandwich (a foam-rubber prop with green cotton hanging out of it to represent lettuce); the sound technician has forgotten to bring the telephone tape after having spent an hour phoning her best friend so she could record busy signals and ringing sounds; the lead actor is sick. Yes, it's hectic...but a lot of fun.

"Bravo!"

All actors want the sound of applause ringing in their ears as they take their bows. It's also a boost to get rave reviews in writing.

When the performances are finished, the sets struck, and the classroom "back to normal," ask students to write notes of applause. Provide colourful paper, cut into various sizes. Some people will be brief in their compliments:

The musical breaks between scenes were so cool. Matched the mood of murder.

To – The Phantoms

You were the awesomest director

Sandy.

Others will be more verbose:

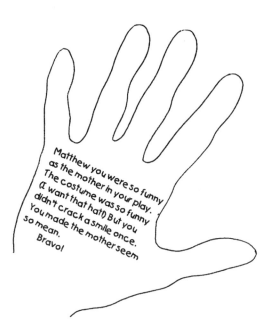

When these notes are on display, it's an inviting bulletin of compliments. Some students might draw their own hand shape on paper, then write their "applause" on this, giving the impression of hands clapping.

To encourage lots of compliments, ask that everyone write at least three in order to earn this class credit. Because the notes are on display, they should be proofread by the teacher before being posted. This will give you the chance to teach a quick lesson in spelling or grammar for some and to encourage others to add enough details.

Some of the compliments are directed towards the entire troupe. This helps to avoid the awkwardness of any students being left out. I also write some notes, especially to the troupes. Sometimes, I'll drop a hint to the directors to do the same thing, if they haven't already thought of it.

Evaluation is two-fold in this workshop: writing and performance. For the script, I evaluate, once again, using the five categories: purpose, organization, content, effectiveness, correctness. For the performance, I use different criteria: voice clarity, voice expression, memorization, use of props, movement, costume, and "other." That last category is there to give actors a chance to get value for something they have contributed to the play individually (making scenery, playing more than one role, taping sound effects, etc.). I find it easier to ask students to do a self-evaluation before I do mine.

The posters and the applause displays are there on the walls celebrating everyone long after stage dust has settled.

CHAPTER 10

The thesis paper

Is man an ape or an angel? I am on the side of the angels. I repudiate with indignation and abohorrence those new fangled theories.

BENJAMIN DISRAELI

The first barrier to thesis papers is that ominous word "THESIS" — it seems to growl from a dark cave, threatening thinkers. So, never underestimating the control of language over thought, I avoid that word for as long as I can.

ROMEO AND JULIET as a sample study

Usually, in high school English courses, thesis papers are assigned in connection with a major study, for example, of a novel or of a play. Since a recent grade 11 study of *Romeo and Juliet* is fresh in my mind as I write, let me describe for you the steps through which I led my students towards their thesis papers.

The thesis paper by any other name

Before seeing a film version of the play, we read the prologue and discuss what it suggests about the play. Some students offer their ideas:

"The families are fighting."

"Romeo and Juliet fall in love."

"Romeo and Juliet both die."

"The families feel bad but it's too late."

This is when I begin the journey towards the thesis paper which will be assigned in about five weeks. I ask students: "Do you have any theories about the fighting, or the love, or the deaths?"

When someone asks what a theory is, I get a few people in the class to look up the word in a variety of dictionaries. We hear some definitions until everyone is satisfied that a theory doesn't have to be "right" — it's a guess that is based on some evidence. Each student then writes a theory about *Romeo and Juliet* in their own journal:

"They die because that's the only way they can be together."

"The families are fighting to control Verona."

"The fighting stops because everyone's too sad to fight."

"Someone kills Romeo and Juliet for revenge."

Let the play begin!

We've begun to think about the play and now we're ready to watch it. It takes several classes for us to view the whole play, so I make sure there is time at the beginning and end of each period for casual talk. Students are asked to write brief notes in their journals, too: what confuses you? what do you think might happen? what did you find interesting?

At the end of Act 1, I ask: Do you have any theories about why these two people fall in love?

"Love at first sight."

"Romeo's on the rebound."

"Juliet's afraid of how her parents want her to get married so she's just making sure she gets the guy she wants and can't marry the other guy her parents want."

"It's not love, it's lust."

I still have not mentioned the ominous THESIS PAPER. But people are listening to each other's theories and beginning to argue.

More time to think

Part of the study of the play, after our viewing of the film, involves creating a storyboard. This year, I had three classes of grade 11s. Divided into teams of five, they were assigned to contribute a few scenes to the storyboard. The result is that the entire play becomes a colourful, clearly labeled storyboard display in our room. This is a valuable focus for all our talk and inquiry.

Theories, theories, theories

We discuss the concept of power: where does it come from? what makes it last? who had power in this play? Then I ask: do you have any theories about who held the most power in *Romeo and Juliet*? Again, a journal entry is made by each student.

We look at many of the decisions made in the play (these are marked by large gold stars placed by students in the appropriate scenes on the storyboard). I ask: Do you have any theories about which decision was the most crucial to the outcome of this play? Another journal entry.

We discuss blame: what is blame? who decides blame? Do you have any theories about blame in connection with the deaths of Romeo and Juliet?

Christopher Columbus and the thesis paper

By now, students have six or seven theories. It's time to talk about Christopher Columbus. He had a theory about the shape of the earth and he convinced others to agree with him. Eventually, his theory was proven to be fact — no longer arguable.

I ask students to look back over all the theories which they have written during the past few weeks: have any been proven to be fact? or can you still imagine someone arguing with you, "No, the world is not flat!"?

Now, we're getting precariously close to the thesis paper. I'm extra careful at this point, or they'll see through the trick of vocabulary to discover that "monster" lurking.

Taking a strong first step

I ask students to choose one theory that interests them, one for which they can clearly see their own strong arguments. Then, I ask them to imagine someone else sitting across from them, arguing the opposite view. If they can refute that view, they have a workable theory. They write and submit statements for my comment.

A few are not theories, but are facts:

"Romeo killed himself because he couldn't live without Juliet."

"The Friar said the deaths were his fault."

Some are vague theories:

"I think that the most important decision was the fighting."

"Parents shouldn't try to run their children's lives."

Many are strong theories:

"Blind trust in religion is the reason Romeo and Juliet died."

"Tybalt's personality caused all the deaths because of the fact he was one of those weak-character, strong-fighter types."

The toughest job is finished

When I return these theories, they are marked as "insightful," "thoughtful," "clear," or "in progress." Only that fourth comment would require some extra help from me. The majority of students will have "clear" thesis statements, and several will have "thoughtful" ones. A few will delve into the depths of thinking to produce an "insightful" thesis statement.

When everyone has a theory which is strong and well-worded, I let the "monster" out of the cave and assign the thesis paper on *Romeo and Juliet*. By now, though, after roughly two classes of discussion and thought, it's not a monster at all.

Focusing thought before writing

The thesis statement is only the beginning, of course. Now it's time to make detailed connections between the words in the thesis statement and the play itself. The handout on the next page has been designed to help students focus before writing.

There are moans and some loud protests. Yet, for most students, this simple outline is not threatening. They easily see that they've already begun thinking through their arguments. For some, I need to encourage them by stating the opposite of their theory, forcing them to argue with me.

One classroom experience

Deeone has put her pen down and crossed her arms. "I can't do this. I never wrote a thesis paper before."

"But you're already started," I say. "The toughest job is done. You have your thesis statement."

"I don't like it."

That stops me for a minute. She had written a clear theory about how unquestioning faith in the Friar was to blame for the deaths of the two lovers. Now she's telling me she can't write that paper because she's not interested in it. She's right.

"So, tell me, Deeone, is there something about these lovers that you find interesting? Got any theories about them?"

"Well, it might not make much sense to you."

"Try me."

"It's sort of stupid. But I'll say it anyways. What I think made them both think they were in love is that they weren't allowed to be. I mean, ask anyone and they'll tell you that if parents say they can't do something then they want to do it."

THESIS PAPER

A "theory" is an educated guess. A person speculates on a certain topic after having done some research and some thinking. A "thesis" is a written work about this theory. A person writes an argument in which he/she attempts to convince others that the "guess" is actually "a truth." Evidence for this theory comes from the research. The writer explains the evidence and connects it clearly to the theory.

THESIS PAPER OUTLINE

Theory (or the basic argument):

_____

_____

_____

Evidence (make four/five points, through research):

_____

_____

_____

_____

Specific Evidence (find quotes to back up your main ideas):

_____

_____

_____

_____

I try an argument. "No one would fake themselves into believing they're in love just to defy parents. No way."

Deeone lifts herself up from a slouch. "Yes they would. Like when her mother tells her about marrying that Paris guy and she hasn't even thought about getting married. She's only thirteen so her mother still thinks she can boss her around."

"Well I think all thirteen-year-olds pretty well do what their parents say."

"Oh boy, you're wrong there. I should know." She rolls her eyes. "My parents and I fight bad enough now, but boy when I was thirteen it was like war."

I can see that her new thesis paper is on the way.

Next day, she's back again. "What kind of quotes am I supposed to get?"

We go to the storyboard and I ask her to point to the places mentioned in her outline. Part of the job of creating the storyboard had been for each expert group to choose a single quote to best represent the scene they depicted.

"Do you see any quotes that help to prove you're right?"

She chooses one, then starts flipping through her text, glancing up at the storyboard from time to time. "I need something from when her father yelled at her. That was pretty bad. He practically told her she should die."

Soon, all her quotes are chosen.

Within ten minutes, though, her hand is in the air. "But how do I make this into a whole long paper? It'll be boring."

"Just write it the same way you were arguing with me yesterday. When it starts to sound boring, stop and cut stuff out because if you're bored, I'll be bored."

"You mean just sound like talking?"

"Yea, like talking."

Crayons as a thinking tool

A few days later, all rough drafts are due. I distribute crayons, two per student. "Colour in the main point of your paper — your thesis statement."

We talk about where this statement has been placed in relation to the whole paper, and why. Some students volunteer to read aloud their words written before the thesis statement and they think out loud about whether these introductory words add interest or slow down the paper. I see a few people crossing out lines, while others add more to their opening paragraphs.

"Now, with that same colour shade in every one of your own ideas which connects to this opening statement. Take that second crayon and shade in every part which is an example taken from the play to back up your ideas."

The crayons slide back and forth across the pages. Some students hold their crayons thoughtfully, colouring in very little. I notice that Deeone is busy adding yellow and blue, switching crayons in a nice balance of color.

"Look back at everything that is not shaded in and make a decision as to whether this adds to your arguments or not. If not, cut it."

This simple visual device gives me an opportunity to see who might need help focusing on their topic and who does not, who has a balance of arguments with examples and who does not.

Students seem to enjoy the childlike act of colouring as they re-think. It's reassuring when I hear someone say, "Check this out. No white patches." But there's the occasional "Oh man, nothing's coloured in after my first page."

Revisiting, revising

Next, I ask students to look back at their outlines, numbering each argument they had intended to present. Then, they read through their papers, putting corresponding numbers on every paragraph, thinking about organization as they work.

By now, the pages are colourful and quite a mess.

Dictionaries are distributed, and students read through once again, underlining any words that might not be spelled correctly. In pairs, they double-check each other's writing.

More mess.

At this point, some are ready to begin a final draft, others are making more changes, while a few need appointments for extra help. The colouring and the numbering seem to work for most people, even those whose papers hadn't been focused at all.

Thesis papers as entertainment

Before class ends, I remind students to find a reader for their final draft. Because I have been inside the process for so long and because my job is to evaluate the thesis papers, I am aware that I cannot provide what every writer needs — a reader who is seeing their work for the first time. So, once again, reader response sheets are distributed so that every writer can have a fresh reaction:

We have come full circle again in the writing process, giving time, building confidence, supporting with instruction, and finding a meaningful audience.

When students submit their thesis papers for evaluation by me (once again, I use the five evaluation categories), I ask that they put their outlines, rough drafts, final drafts, and reader responses in their folders. This gives them an opportunity to consider the whole process as they organize their folders; and it gives me a chance to give credit for everything.

"You writing is very effective and intelligently writing. You express yourself nobly write and I feel as though you are speaking directly to me when I read your writing. You expressed great views!"

Tina

"I know what you mean about how families can do more harm than good by trying to dictate their children's lives. Good job, Ryan."

Mom

89

A *literary feast*

We read to understand, or begin to understand. We cannot
do but read.

ALBERTO MANGUEL

Are you hungry? Come to our Literary Feast and satisfy your appe-
tite for words!

We've rearranged the desks and tables of the classroom into a
banquet semi-circle. Balloons are floating their colours — blue, pur-
ple, yellow, red. The tables are spread with delectable writings by
student authors.

During the past months, students have been creating and crafting
their poetry and prose. We're ready for more readers!

The Literary Feast

Our Literary Feast is a three-day event which celebrates the
writer-reader partnership. It is not a competition. All students who
are willing to write, revise, rewrite, and share are included. Everyone who wants to read a little or a lot is invited to come to the Feast
as often as they wish.

What does the Literary Feast look like?

On the "banquet table," folders are displayed in general alphabetical sections (by author). There is one folder for each writer or for each group of writers who may, for example, have worked together to create a play or a magazine.

The folder itself serves to introduce the writer to the readers. Each one has an author profile written on the outside and is decorated with drawings, photographs, or magazine pictures. The profile can be a formal, brief biography of the writer, or it can be in a style all its own: a recipe of ingredients that make up the author; a poem to show some aspects of the writer's life; a "lost and found" ad.

Personalizing the writing folder

Each folder is an invitation to read. Richie has written a series of vignettes about his many second-hand vehicles. On his folder is a photograph of his latest purchase — a bright red truck.

Tanya has made a collage of magazine pictures and words that represent her: volleyball, fashion, friends, kittens.

Bradon, who is eighteen, has his baby picture next to his author profile. He writes about how poetry just comes to him when he isn't even thinking about it, especially in chemistry class.

Getting the word out

Posters inviting everyone to our Literary Feast are displayed around the school and notices are sent home in our school newsletter. Teachers book their classes to spend a period or two at the Feast.

Many students from other English courses in our school add their folders to the display — the more the better!

The mood of the Feast

There is a kind of hush at the Literary Feast. Not a silence, but a quiet that takes this classroom out of the ordinary and creates something new. Sometimes there are only a few students in the room, while at other times there are fifty or more. Still, there is that quiet.

People browse the tables, perhaps looking for friends' writing, and sometimes curious to read the work of someone they don't know. It's an informal atmosphere.

Some "snapshots" of a Literary Feast

Scott leans across the table and says to Aaron, "Hey, check this out. It's Bradon's."

Aaron looks at the folder. "What'd he write? Something about basketball I bet."

"No." Scott sounds dubious. "It's poems."

Maxine, cross-legged on the floor, doesn't even notice the dozens of feet that walk past. She's chewing on a fingernail, reading Tanya's Dracula story. She's on page six where Damon, as he dances with Tamara, feels his two teeth ache and change shape.

Over in a corner, three boys have pulled their chairs together and Brett is reading out loud a magazine article, written by Mark, about sexual abstinence. "Mark's crazy," one of them says. The others laugh nervously.

Suddenly, Allalie bursts out laughing. She's reading Jevon's composition about a day when everything went wrong. He has a way of splicing fact and fiction together, with terrific timing for an unexpected punchline.

Allalie reads a passage to Candace. When Candace starts to laugh, Alex walks over to find out what's so funny. Reading the passage again, out of breath, tears run down Allalie's face.

Shane and Matthew are late for class. "What's going on?" says Shane as they walk into the room.

"It's that Feast thing," says Matthew with as much interest as one could thread through the eye of a needle.

They both go to a window and stare out for a while.

I invite them to the party. "Sit and relax with a good read, you guys. Lots of interesting stuff here."

They take the hint and amble past the Feast tables, but don't actually look at any folders. Just when I begin to get discouraged, Matthew stops. He reaches for a folder with a group picture on it: six grade 12s have written a magazine called "*Anarchy.*"

Shane follows Matthew back to some chairs near the window. Matthew silently reads "*Anarchy*" while Shane looks outside. I keep watching over the top of my pen as I write a postcard to Jason about his essay on Winston Churchill.

And then, what I had been hoping for happens: Matthew leans towards Shane and points to a page. He reads aloud. Shane doesn't actually turn away from the window. Not at first. He just glances back over his shoulder, listening. But now he wants to look closer at something. So he pulls his chair over beside Matthew's, and they are reading "*Anarchy*" together.

I turn my attention away from them and back to the Churchill essay. Next, I pick up Jed's fantasy comic. Great artwork! Excellent suspense!

Postcards and mail call

Near the classroom door is a large, decorated mailbox. Blank postcards are stacked there for readers to jot short notes to the authors. And lots of people use them. This year, almost 800 postcards were delivered over the three-day period.

Reading some mail

Owen wrote to Karolyn: "You have a great mind for thinking. Your writings are excellent. Keep up the good work."

Karolyn's mom, during the evening open house, wrote: "Keep your mind open and busy. Continue to write what you feel. You have great vocabulary. Have some fun!"

Dan sent a postcard to Kerri Ann: "I really enjoyed your poetry,

Literary Feast

Title of writing: _____

Name of writer: _____

_____

_____

_____

_____

_____

from _____

which is an extreme compliment considering the fact that as a poet, I am quite critical when it comes to other people's poetry. An interesting writing style which is free from pretension."

Lisa's card to Daphne said: "Your poetry is AWESOME!! I can't believe you can write so good! It just flows so freely ... very emotional."

Roxanne, who is in grade 10 and is displaying her writing for the first time, sent a postcard to a senior student, Kathryn: "I liked your poem called 'Pain'. I know what you mean because I felt that way too. I write a lot if I'm depressed. Do you?"

Setting up a postal service

A team of students help me to sort the mail each day. We read each postcard to make sure there are no unkind notes — four were discarded out of the 800 this year.

At the beginning of each class, I deliver the mail, one of the special treats of the Literary Feast. Authors try in vain to cover their excitement as I call out their names to pick up their postcards. Some will read the notes to friends, and some will let me read cards aloud to the class. Others tuck them away, privately.

Author readings

Last year, we had two public readings of student writing: one at noonhour and one in the evening. Six to eight students read each time to small audiences of about thirty, the usual intimate crowd for author readings. There were shy introductions by each writer, some speaking about where their ideas came from or perhaps telling about why they like to write. Whole stories were read, or poems, or excerpts from longer pieces. The sound of the applause each time was like an award.

This spring, I did not include those readings in our Feast, feeling somehow busier than usual and not able to orchestrate it all. I'm disappointed about that now.

But next year...

ACKNOWLEDGEMENTS

In developing my own writing as well as my career as a teacher of writing, I have gained so much from collaboration and from workshops with writers and teachers. I wish to acknowledge the contribution of some of these people to my own learning:

Janet Barkhouse, Dr. Anthony Barton, Ann Blackwood, Susan Church, George Elliott Clarke, Rhonda Himmelman, Joan James, Anne MacLean, Alistair MacLeod, Eli Mandel, W.O. Mitchell, Alice Munro, and Dorothy Perkyns.

5161